UP CLOSE

Killer Spiders

PAUL HARRISON

FRANKLIN WATTS
LONDON·SYDNEY

Published in 2009 by Franklin Watts

Copyright © 2009 Arcturus Publishing Limited

Franklin Watts
338 Euston Road
London NW1 3BH

Franklin Watts Australia
Level 17/207 Kent Street
Sydney, NSW 2000

Author: Paul Harrison
Editor: Kate Overy
Designers: Trevor Cook, Sally Henry

Picture credits: Flagstaffotos: 14 bottom, 16 bottom;
Frank Lane Picture Agency: 5 top, 20 bottom; Joao. P.
Burini: 8 top; Nature Picture Library: 12 top and
bottom; Photolibrary: title page, 4 bottom, 9 bottom,
15 left and right, 16 top, 19 right; Photoshot: cover, 20
bottom, 21 top; Rex Features: 6 bottom, 7 bottom;
Science Photo Library: 5 bottom, 10 top and bottom,
18 top and bottom, 21 bottom.

A CIP catalogue record for this book is available from
the British Library

Dewey number: 595.4

ISBN: 978-0-7496-9215-5
SL000953EN

Printed in China

Franklin Watts is a division of Hachette Children's
Books, an Hachette UK Company
www.hachette.co.uk

Contents

Bits and Pieces

Spiders have been around for over 300 million years. There are at least 35,000 species. They are expert hunters, trapping their *prey* and killing it with their venomous fangs.

FANGTASTIC

Spiders inject *venom* through their fangs. Many spiders have fangs big enough to pierce human flesh. Some can even bite through shoes!

LOVELY LEGS

Spiders have eight legs with six joints in each. They have the ability to grow a new leg if they lose one.

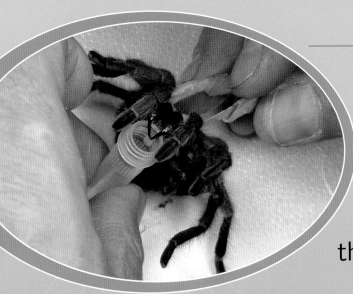

NASTY STUFF

Spiders keep their venom in two *glands*, just behind their fangs. Spiders don't always use their venom. Sometimes they bite as a warning.

Some spiders can have up to four pairs of eyes.

WEBBED WONDER

Most spiders have *spinnerets* at the rear of their bodies to produce silk for making webs. Spider silk is very tough – it's stronger than steel!

5

Deadly Effect

Different spiders have different types of venom. Fortunately, only 25 of over 35,000 kinds of spider have venom that can harm humans.

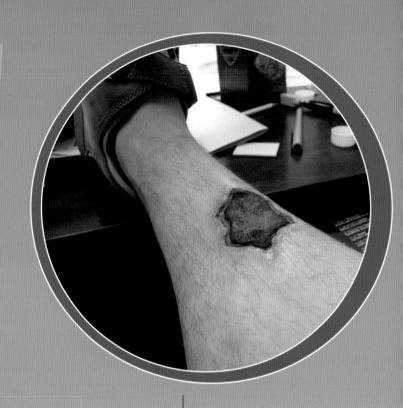

JAWS OF DEATH

A spider bite can put you into a *coma*, *paralyse* you, or damage major organs of the body.

DEAD LEG

Often people don't realise that a spider has bitten them. Sometimes the first thing they see is bruising or blistering around the bite holes. In extreme cases, the skin around the affected area will turn black and die.

HOT SHOTS

A bite from a deadly spider doesn't always lead to death. Even the most poisonous spider bites can be treated with antivenin – an *antidote* that overcomes the effects of the venom.

LIFELINE

The quicker a victim can be treated with antivenin, the better their chance of survival. It also helps if you can identify the spider. In 2005, a Brazilian wandering spider bit a chef in Somerset, England. Luckily, he took a photograph of it, which helped doctors save his life.

01-04-05_2118
Size: 5.75Kb

BACK   DETAILS

Spider venom can be useful – it is used as a pesticide and can help cure brain damage.

UNWELCOME WANDERER

The Brazilian wandering spider is one of the most venomous spiders in the world. It bites more people each year than any other venomous spider.

WAITING GAME

Australian funnel web spiders wait in small burrows for their next meal to pass by. The Sydney funnel web is particularly dangerous to humans. Over 13 deaths were directly linked to its bites in the last 10 years.

When it bites, the funnel web nearly always delivers a full dose of venom.

8

Hairy Horrors

Deadly spiders are not usually as big and hairy as we might imagine. But the tarantula is both!

OLD AND NEW

There are two different types of tarantula: those found in the Old World (Africa and Asia), and those from the New World (the Americas). There are over 900 species of tarantula.

BIG APPETITES

The world's biggest spider – the goliath bird-eating spider – is a kind of tarantula. It can grow to over 30 centimetres (12 inches) across. It eats birds, frogs and even small snakes.

HAIR-RAISING

If a New World tarantula feels threatened, it will rub its back legs together, then kick and flick its barbed hairs at the target. The hairs have small hooks on them that stick to the skin and can cause irritation.

Some tarantulas have retractable claws, just like cats!

DANGEROUS?

It's unusual for a New World tarantula to bite a human. Old World tarantulas use biting for defence, especially if provoked. A bite from an Old World tarantula can be very dangerous.

THE INSECTS REVENGE

Among the enemies of the tarantula, the nastiest is the spider wasp. The female wasp paralyses the spider by stinging it. Then she digs a hole, or uses the spider's own, and puts the spider and an egg into it. Later, the egg hatches and the wasp *larva* eats away at the paralysed spider.

ANGRY ARACHNID

A tarantula uses its size to ward off potential *predators*. It may rear up on its back legs to make itself look bigger and scarier. Some tarantulas can even make a noise. The predator usually runs away!

Ambush Attack

Some spiders use their venom with extra cunning to hunt their prey.

TRAPDOOR TERROR

Trapdoor spiders live in burrows covered by a camouflaged trapdoor. They lie in wait underground for the sound of their prey. As the victim gets close, the trapdoor spider leaps out of its burrow. Its prey can be anything from insects to baby frogs, baby snakes, mice – even small fish!

MADE YOU JUMP

The jumping spider stalks its prey, and then pounces on it from several inches away. It takes its victim by surprise! It has a very painful bite but it's only mildly poisonous for humans.

MUM'S THE WORD

The female hobo spider becomes very aggressive when a human gets too close to its egg sac, the webby enclosure which contains its eggs. If you come across its funnel-like web keep well clear to avoid a bite.

A spider eats around 2,000 insects every year.

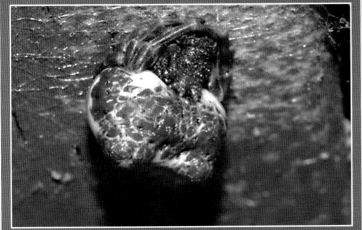

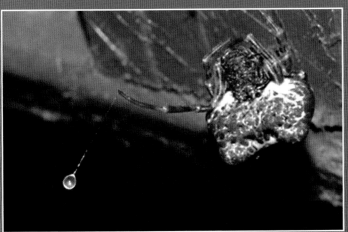

CATCH YOU LATER

The bolas spider spends the daytime on the upper surface of a leaf, disguised as a bird dropping. At night it moves to the underside of the leaf, and makes a sticky blob of web on the end of a line. It uses it to catch moths as they pass nearby. It is also called an angling or fishing spider.

WALK THIS WAY

The crab spider looks like a crab and can move like one, running sideways or backwards. Crab spiders do not build webs to trap prey, but are hunters and ambushers. Some species sit inside flowers, where they grab visiting insects.

Sometimes the trapdoor spider strikes so quickly, it grabs inedible victims by mistake.

MOUSE HOUSE

The mouse spider gets its name from its habit of living in burrows, like the trapdoor spider. It uses similar techniques to catch its prey. It is very timid and unlikely to bite a human. Some species carry highly toxic venom. Male mouse spiders are fast enough to run down their prey. They leave their burrows in search of a mate. Females are deadlier and stay at home, underground – unless they're accidentally disturbed.

Small but Nasty

They say that big surprises come in small packages. This is especially true in the world of venomous spiders!

RED WARNING

The Australian redback spider is easy to spot because of its bright red markings. It is a relative of the American black widow and is just as *lethal*.

WIDOW MAKER

The female black widow spider is only around 1.5 centimetres (about half an inch) across the body but its venom is many times more powerful than a rattlesnake's.

BAD HABIT

When the spitting spider gets close to its prey, it spits a gluey substance, a combination of venom and web. This stops the prey in its tracks. The spider can then kill and eat the unfortunate insect at its leisure.

Female black widow spiders sometimes kill and then eat the male after mating.

FALSE REPUTATION?

The white-tailed spider of Australia has a reputation for giving people painful bites. In fact, the worst of these probably come from a different spider altogether.

JUMPING ANTS?

Many kinds of spider mimic other species, either to escape predators or to get closer to their prey. Some small jumping spiders imitate ants, and carry one pair of legs like antennae. The spider ant can jump many times its own body length to capture its prey.

DROP IN SOMETIME

The tiny sheet weaver or money spider constructs a flat sticky web, often on leaf litter. To its prey it's just as deadly as its bigger cousins.

The smallest spider is thought to be the patu marplesi from Western Samoa. You could fit 10 of them on the end of a pencil!

On the Run

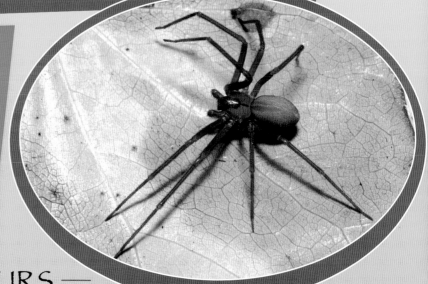

Not all spiders lie in wait for their prey. Some actively pursue their meal — by hunting it!

FORTY-EIGHT HOURS —

The brown *recluse* spider of the United States builds its web for resting in, but doesn't use it to catch prey. It's not aggressive, but can bite if it feels threatened. It's venomous enough to kill a person, but if you live 48 hours after being bitten, you will probably survive.

ON THE HUNT

Huntsman spiders can run fast on their long legs and ambush their prey. They have a 'cling on' *reflex* if they're handled, making it more likely for them to bite. Thankfully, their venom is fairly mild.

The yellow sac spider's favourite food is other spiders. It also bites humans quite often. Its powerful fangs can easily penetrate human skin, but its venom isn't deadly.

THRILL OF THE CHASE

Wolf spiders are venomous enough to be able to eat cane toads, which are up to 30 times the size of the spider. Fortunately for us, wolf spiders would rather run than bite someone, and even if they did bite a person it is unlikely that the effects would be worse than a few days' discomfort.

19

Nasty Surprises

W ith their natural urge to explore, it's hardly surprising that spiders turn up in the most unlikely places!

SUPERMARKET SHOCK

The Brazilian wandering spider likes to rest in shady places – like inside bunches of bananas. Occasionally these turn up in supermarkets where the spider reappears and terrifies an unsuspecting shopper.

Some cultures have been eating spiders for years! It's said they taste nutty and sticky – a bit like peanut butter.

TOILET TALES

Scary stories of people being bitten on the bottom whilst sitting on lavatories are quite common. Thankfully these stories are most definitely urban legends.

HOUSE OF HORRORS

A spider in a house will act like a spider in the wild, so it will look for a dark place to rest. This might mean in an attic, a linen cupboard, or even in a bed.

DON'T HAVE NIGHTMARES

Remember, only very few spiders are deadly to humans and believe it or not, they're all more scared of you than you are of them.

Glossary

Antidote
Medicine taken to work against a poison

Coma
Deep unconsciousness, often as a result of injury

Gland
Part of an animal that makes a particular chemical

Larva
Worm-like young insect that has left the egg but has yet to change to adult form

Lethal
Enough to cause death

Paralyse
Cause part of the body to become incapable of movement

Predator
An animal that catches, kills and eats other animals

Prey
Animal killed by another for food

Recluse
Avoids others and lives alone

Reflex
Action taken in response to something without thought

Spinneret
Organ a spider uses to produce silk for thread or web

Venom
Poisonous fluid produced by animals such as scorpions, snakes and spiders and injected into prey or enemies

Further Reading

Deadly Spiders and Scorpions
Andrew Solway, Heinemann Library
(Wild Predators series), 2004

Spiders
Rebecca Gilpin, Usborne Publishing
(Usborne Beginners series), 2007

Scary Spiders
Lynn Huggins-Cooper, Franklin Watts
(Killer Nature series), 2005

Spider
David Jeffries and Tony Allen, Steck
Vaughn (Killer Creatures series), 2001

Spiders and Their Kin
Herbert and Larna Levi, St Martin's
Press (Golden Guides series) 2001

Spiders and Their Webs
Darlyne A. Murawski, National
Geographic Children's Books, 2004

Spiders of North America
Ann O. Squire, Franklin Watts (Animals
in Order series), 2000

**100 Things You Should Know About
Insects and Spiders**
Steve Parker, Miles Kelly Publishing,
2004

Index